Edmund Burke, Gilbert Wakefield

A Reply to the Letter of Edmund Burke, Esq. to a Noble Lord

Edmund Burke, Gilbert Wakefield

A Reply to the Letter of Edmund Burke, Esq. to a Noble Lord

ISBN/EAN: 9783337064655

Printed in Europe, USA, Canada, Australia, Japan

Cover: Foto ©ninafisch / pixelio.de

More available books at **www.hansebooks.com**

A

REPLY

TO THE LETTER OF

EDMUND BURKE, Esq.

TO A

NOBLE LORD.

By GILBERT WAKEFIELD, B. A.
Late Fellow of Jefus-College, Cambridge.

A NEW EDITION.

Nunc face fuppofitâ fervefcit fanguis, et irâ
Scintillant oculi; dicisque, facisque, quod ipfe
Non fani effe hominis non fanus juret Oreftes.
PERSIUS.

Alafs! not dazzled with their noon-tide ray,
Compute the morn and evening to the day,
The whole amount of this enormous fame,
A tale, that blends their glory with their fhame.
POPE.

PRINTED FOR THE AUTHOR,
AND SOLD BY G. KEARSLEY, NO. 46, FLEET-STREET.

1796.

A

REPLY, &c.

ERRATA.

P. 5. l. 7. from the bottom; for *readers*, read *venders*.

P. 46. l. 11. read: *all the artillery of—Heaven against France:* omitting the words in the parenthesis.

when, I say, this degenerate son of Chatham, with his puny assessors on the treasury-bench, was accustomed, in all the plenitude of official insolence sublimed by all the acrimony of baffled malice, to receive with groans and hisses the rapturous eloquence of EDMUND BURKE, an eloquence that would have charmed the Bacchanals of Thrace to gentleness and humanity; I felt those risings of inexpressible indignation, which an exhibition of unrivalled

B   Genius

A

REPLY, &c.

SOME years ago, when the fon of Chatham, who has reverfed with ignoble accuracy that affecting circumftance of the poet,

—— Dignus patriis qui lætior effet
Imperiis, et cui pater haud Mezentius effet;

when, I fay, this degenerate fon of Chatham, with his puny affeffors on the treafury-bench, was accuftomed, in all the plenitude of official infolence fublimed by all the acrimony of baf-fled malice, to receive with groans and hiffes the rapturous eloquence of EDMUND BURKE, an eloquence that would have charmed the Bacchanals of Thrace to gentlenefs and hu-manity; I felt thofe rifings of inexpreffible in-dignation, which an exhibition of unrivalled

B   Genius

Genius and confummate Virtue, fpurned by the hoofs of Venality and Barbarifm, would excite in the bofom of Senfibility. Some ebullitions of refentment, fome fallies of vexation, fome digreffions of complacent vanity, fhould have been conceded to a long career of patriotic fervices, to extraordinary accomplifhments of intellect, to an univerfal elegance of literature, and to a confpicuous, but pardonable, confcioufnefs of high defert. All but barbarians, unknown to letters and eftranged from humanity, would have weighed the failings of the man with the fupreme endowments of the orator, and have found thofe but as the duft of the balance in competition. A youthful tribe, juft emancipated from fcholaftic difcipline, might have reflected alfo, if unimpreffed by better motives, on thofe ingenuous times of virtuous antiquity, when a precedency of years claimed, and received, the veneration of a father *. But fcanty was their virtue, and " ears to rapture"

---

* Credebant hoc grande nefas; et morte piandum,
Si juvenis vetulo non affurrexerat, et fi
Barbato cuicunque puer ; licet ipfe videret
Plura domi fraga, et majores glandis acervos.
Tam venerabile erat praecedere quatuor annis,
Primaque par adeo facræ lanugo feneflæ.

Juv. xiii. 54.

were

were not their portion. Accordingly, no incident of a similar complexion ever gave me more concern, as far as a sequestered and antiquated student can be suppofed acceffible to such extraneous occurrences, than the defection of Edmund Burke from thofe principles of political attachment, which had regulated the tenour of his life, and conftituted the materials of his glory. For myfelf, I have ever been inclined to put a conftruction on this reverfe of conduct, that fhould encroach with lefs inroad on his virtue, than men of fentiments congenial with my own. I confidered what qualification fhould be made in behalf of a wounded fpirit, indignant at the ingratitude and infenfibility of his fellow-citizens, who could abandon their faithful leaders in the decline of influence, and haften with the mercenary falutations of fervility to " the rifing morn." I conceived, that the dereliction of his plan was partly imputable to a deficiency in the genuine love of truth, and partly to an operation of falfe fhame, not poffeffed of fufficient magnanimity to retract thofe indefenfible pofitions, extorted from a better judgement by the impetuofity of paffion, the offspring of inftantaneous vexation on that irritability of temper, which is too frequently in infeparable concomitant of refined feeling and exalt-

B 2   ed

ed genius. His fituation reminded me of the unhappy mother, in the poet:

Και μανθανω μεν οια τολμησω κακα,
Θυμος δε κρεισσων των εμων βελευματων *.

But, as William Whifton fomewhere fays in his memoirs, with his cuftomary franknefs and fimplicity, that he took frequent opportunities of expoftulating with the Bifhops, and reproving them, for their repeated marriages, in violation forfooth! of the exprefs injunctions of the *apoftolical conflitutions*; and received but *fmall thanks* for his pains: fo many will be difpofed to cherifh

Eurip. Med. 1078, which, for the benefit of the country gentlemen, who have not enjoyed fuch opportunities of learning Greek as my Lord Belgrave and I, may be reprefented in the words of Ovid:

Sed trahit invitam nova vis; aliudque cupido,
Mens aliud fuadet. Video meliora, proboque;
Deteriora fequor. Met. vii. 19.

and for the accommodation of thofe, who live ftill more remote, at the extremities of Wales or the north of Scotland, I fhall fubjoin principally the fimple verfion of Tate and Stoneftreet:

A ftrong defire my yielding foul invades;
And paffion this, and confcience that perfuades.
I fee the right, and I approve it too;
Condemn the wrong, and yet the wrong purfue.

no very elevated conception of my candour in this conftruction on the political deportment of Mr. Burke. That he is chargeable, however, with a relinquilhment of his eftablilhed political character, not only in my opinion, but the judgement of the world at large, is demonftrable, I think, from one indifputable fact. " Who " reads Bolingbroke now? Who ever did read " him through? He is gone to the vault of all " the Capulets:" or equivalent words, were the lively farcaftic triumph of our accomplilhed writer over the deiftical remains of that renowned nobleman. I alfo may fay, " Who reads " Burke? Who ever has read him through?" His mighty quartos, replete as they are with all the illuminations of philofophic truth, with all the enchanting extravagances of the brighteft fancy, with the fpangles of metaphor, the coruf-cations of wit, and the blaze of eloquence ; thefe quartos, I fay, with their inexhauftible ftores of inftruction, delight, and rapture, lie neglected on the fhelf, an incumbrance to the readers, the receptacle of cobwebs, and the feaft of worms. Yet the folution of this extraordinary phænome-non is obvious and unqueftionable. The new To-ries and *old Whigs*, the prefent admirers and parti fans of Mr. Burke, can take no pleafure in " his " tales of other times," in the thunder of that

B 3   oratory,

oratory, which was once launched by him and his compatriots at the devoted head of Lord North and the abettors of American fubjugation ; nor in thofe axioms of conftitutional liberty and political juftice, breathing benevolence to mankind, and raifing the philanthropy of their author to the fublime level of his intellect. This clafs of readers are confronted in every page with pofitions and principles, that were never *theirs*, and are now no longer *his.* They are offended by the hoftilities of argument in the *writer*, and feel themfelves unable to fupprefs the filent impulfe of indignant nature and revolting virtue at the enormous inconfiftency of the *man*, on contrafting his prefent exercitations with his former efforts *. The *new Whigs* are too violently irritated by the fenfe of his defertion to contemplate with complacency in his works the abdicated tenets of a loft, deferted patriot. Thus, between both parties, thefe fruits of genius are abandoned altogether, and fleep in peace, waiting the removal of the prefent occupants, when, upon eafier terms to the phlegmatic purchafer, they will, without the feafonable charms of novelty,

---

* Hei mihi ! qualis erat, quantum mutatus ab illo
Hectore !
If thou beeft he—but oh ! how fall'n ! how chang'd
From him— !

Demand

Demand new bodies, and in calf's array,
Rush to the world, impatient for the day.

Ask the bookfellers: they will shake their heads,
and confirm my statement. These ill-fated volumes may be suitably compared, with respect
to the present and paft admirers of Mr. Burke,
to the punishments of Mezentius:

Mortua quin etiam jungebat corpora vivis,
Componens manibusque manus, atque oribus ora.

For the *later* writings of our author are to
one the putrid carcafe, that is unfavoury in
their noftrils, and contaminates their enjoyment; his *former* writings are that carcafe to
the other. This mighty genius was once the
admiration of *both* parties for his eloquence and
his virtue: he is certainly this day but the
darling of *one* at moft, for his eloquence alone.

Befides, an indifference to truth, or at leaft but
a dull perception of her charms, is not obfcurely
intimated even by the title of one book, *An Af-
peal from the New to the Old Whigs*. The firft
queftion, obvious and natural, which I afked,
when I read this title, and which Mr. Burke
fhould have afked himfelf before he wrote it,
was: " Of what comparative importance are

B 4   " the

" the fentiments of the *old Whigs*, or of the
" *new ?*" The proper inquiry, in every inftance,
is this alone, " Where is truth, moral and
" political,. to be found ?" With *arguments* furely,
and not with *nofes*. It appears to me, that fomething is effentially wrong in the intellectual conftitution of that writer, who makes his Gothic
appeal to the fallible judgements of a party ; and
weighs, not the cogency of reafons, but the ex-
ternal characters of men.

After thefe preliminary obfervations, which
may contribute, as their intention is, to con-
vince the reader of my freedom from all perfonal
bias, unfavourable to Mr. Burke, on this occafion ; I proceed to the pamphlet itfelf, which did
not reach me, and that cafually, before this
day, February 26.

" To be ill fpoken of, in whatever language
" they fpeak, by the zealots of the new fect in
" philofophy and politicks, of which thefe no-
" ble perfons think fo charitably, and of which
" others think fo juftly, to me, is no matter of
" uneafinefs or furprife."

Now thefe " zealots of the new fect in philo-
" fophy and politicks," to define them in the
moft

moſt malignant latitude of acceptation, are
thoſe who build on the natural equality of the
human race, and the unaſſailable principles of
univerſal juſtice, the claim of every citizen in a
community, to an equal enjoyment of privilege
and protection, and the reaſonable comforts of
ſociety in proportion to his diligence and worth.
But is this a *new ſect*, and are their *principles* alſo
new? Mr. Burke! you are a ſcholar; well
verſed, I believe, in the writings of the great
geniuſes of antiquity. You are yourſelf comparable, as a man of exuberant conception and
ſplendid eloquence, to the nobleſt of them all.
Will you condeſcend to inform me, in what ce-
lebrated author of Greece or Rome, whether
poet, philoſopher, or hiſtorian, we do not find
ſuch principles of univerſal liberty, blended alike
with an acrimonious abhorrence of ſervility and
uſurpation, inculcated with enthuſiaſtic ardour
and ſedulous anxiety? Shall I remind you of a
ſentiment in Homer, that morning ſtar of literature to the heathen world?

Ἥμισυ γαρ τ'αρετης απααινεται ευρυοπα Ζευς
Ανερος, ευτ' αν μιν κατα δουλιον ημαρ ελησιν *.

* Od. K. 322. Or, as Pope well renders:
Jove fixt it certain, that the fatal day,
Which makes men ſlaves, takes half their worth away.

He

He would have feen, that, in a country like our's, in fpite of thofe *unfpeakable* and *undefcribable* bleffings, a *free parliament,* and a *glorious conftitution* in church and ftate ; he would have feen, I fay, through this fog of nominal impofition and infufferable infult, that the greater part of fociety, who can fcarcely provide for mere animal fubfiftence, are *neceffarily flaves*; mere dependents on the capricious bounties of their fuperiours, and of courfe expofed to all thofe vices, which are connected with abject fubordination, with laborious employments that preclude intellectual improvement, the pureft handmaid of morality! with thofe degrading accommodations, that fink a man in his own efteem, and fhut out the vivifying influence of generous and exalted fentiment.

Again : to pafs over a long lift of illuftrious heroes through many centuries, even Virgil, who was indebted, not for fubfiftence only, but for life, to the favour of an arbitrary prince, never abandoned that magnanimity of foul and rectitude of thought, congenial to a Roman fpirit. He dared to proclaim *the lovelinefs of liberty* in the face of his faviour, his benefactor, and his fovereign :

—— natofque

—— natosque pater, nova bella moventes,
Ad pœnam pulchrâ pro libertate vocabit.
Infelix! Utcumque ferent ea facta minores,
Vincet amor patriæ, laudumque immenfa cupido *.

He not only ftates the fact, you fee, in the garb
of engaging language, but vindicates and extols
the motive : eternifing the father, who doomed
his fons to death for confpiring to reinftate an
exiled monarch in his throne, and diffolve DE-
MOCRACY! Thefe are the heralds of equality and
liberty in ancient times. From Edmund Burke
and the *new Whigs* of our days, I appeal to thefe
antiquated Whigs of Athens and of Rome.

Indeed, I know not, if any topic of medita-
tion has been productive to my mind of more
furprife, and of regret, and fhame, and horrour,
commenfurate to that furprife, than what arifes

---

* Æn. vi. 821. Thus tranflated diffufely, but with incomparable elegance, by Pitt :

His fons, who arm the Tarquins to maintain,
And fix oppreffion in the throne again,
He nobly yields to juftice, in the caufe
Of facred Freedom, and infulted laws.
Though harfh th' unhappy father may appear,
The judge compels the fire to be fevere ;
And the fair hopes of fame the patriot move
To fink the private in the public love.

from

from an obfervation of thofe youths of family and fortune, who have received their education in our public fchools and univerfities. The ftudy of thefe authors in queftion forms the chief occupation of their time : they read the moft approved of them, pregnant with the cœleftial fire of freedom in their fentiments, in all the charms of melodious verfe, and all the prodigality of grand expreffion, even to the folicitude of imprinting them with exaƐt fidelity on their memories; but, ftrange to tell, and hideous to believe! without transfufing the vigour of their precepts into their own lives and converfations. The pure ftream of fober political equality, imbibed at thefe facred fountains, paffes through their bofoms, as the fabulous river through the ocean.*; neither intermingling it's current, nor imparting in the tranfit the flighteft flavour of it's qualities. From the democratical inveƐtives of Demofthenes and the fervid vehemence of Lucan, that true hierophant of liberty, thefe unaccountable votaries of the claffic ages cringe at court with fulfome adulation, fell their fervices of ignominy to a jobbing minifter, and barter for fordid gold their own virtue, the rights of

---

* Sic tibi, cum fluƐtus fubterlabere Sicanos
Doris amara fuam non intermifceat undam

their

their countrymen, and the well-being of the human race.

" It is foothing to my wounded mind, to be
" commended by an able, vigorous, and well-
" informed ftatefman, and at the very moment
" when he ftands forth with a manlinefs and re-
" folution, worthy of himfelf and of his caufe,
" for the prefervation of the perfon and govern-
" ment of our Sovereign, and therein for the fe-
" curity of the laws, the liberties, the morals,
" and the lives of his people."

Suppofe then we vary the direction of our furvey: fuppofe we put on, for the amufement of a few minutes only, our retrofpective fpectacles, and contemplate the vaft atchievements of this wonder-working ftatefman, Lord Grenville, in the bold prominence of irrefragable facts: a ftatefman, whofe infolence, I think, is of a fabric, for obduracy, beyond that of his compatriot and coadjutor, EXISTING CIRCUMSTANCES, I mean, in the Houfe of Commons; who was heretofore my Coryphæus in this refpect, the undoubted and legitimate heir of the Cibberian forehead of our fathers :

The genuine mafter of the *fevenfold face !*

This

This man and his compeers *fet out* with a defign
to partition and plunder France and her domi-
nions; to reftore priefthood to her ftalls, ariftocracy to her privileges, and monarchy to her
throne: he *concludes* his courfe with a willing-
nefs to fign the eternal death-warrant of priefthood, nobility, and royalty in that kingdom,
and to acknowledge the eftablifhment of a republic on their ruins. The only obftacle now is,
(a circumftance fupremely laughable to me, but
tranfcendently ignominious to this paragon of
ftatefmen) not whether France is to be parti-
tioned and conquered, but whether fhe fhall
preferve her conquests!

——————— rifum teneatis, amici ?

The pretended *motives* to this war (for the
real motives were, beyond all controverfy, the
fuppreffion of a reforming fpirit in the focieties
at home, and an actual hoftility againft the happinefs and liberties of Englifhmen) the pretended
motives, I fay, were the prefervation of property
againft republicans and levellers, and the main-
tenance of focial order and religion. The iffue
has been a reduction of his own country to the
extremity of diftrefs, fo as to endanger the very
exiftence of our government, and all property
moft effectually, by the probability in no long
time

time of a national bankruptcy, with or without a continuance of the war ; whilst the poor are perishing in our streets with famine, and placemen, jobbers, and contractors are glutting their insatiable rapacity with the vitals of their agonising country. The *means* also to this issue have been a prodigious complication of crimes and miseries, unexampled in the annals of our species. Europe and the Indies have been converted into one vast slaughter-house, in whose horrid precincts two millions of human beings have been immolated to the Moloch of English ministers, for the preservation truly! of the faith of Jesus, and for the honour of Jehovah! The professors of a religion, which breathes grace, and mercy, and peace, unlimited and undistinguishing, to all the children of mortality, have thundered, at the command of secular superiours, their impious anathemas against French republicans, and poured their imprecations of vengeance and extermination to the Father of all flesh, to the God of love and mercy : that God, who *then*, as those very republicans *now*, " laughed them to scorn, and had them in de-
" rision."

What a reverse is here ! What projects, what means, and what an issue to this series of vast transactions !

tranfa&ions! Is it poffible for the language and
capacities of man to fet forth this fingularity of
events, this wonderful, but glorious, cataftrophe,
in any terms of emphafis and fignificance, beyond the efficacy of an unadorned ftatement?
Were even the domineering talents of Mr.
Burke to exert all their energies in the exhibition of this mighty fubjeēt, we fhould ftill fay,
Materies fuperabat opus! the higheft flights of
eloquence fink beneath the tafk, and are beg-
gared, with all their exaggeration, by the plain
materials. Such, gentle reader! is the refult of
this fame Lord Grenville's political exercitations!
fuch are the bleffed fruits, fuch the incalculable
benefits, of the manlinefs and refolution of this
" able, vigorous, and well-informed ftatefman;"
benefits and bleffings, charaĉterifed by Mr.
Burke himfelf with an unexceptionable accuracy of phrafe, and that ftriĉt propriety of terms,
that extorts even my affent ; as WORTHY OF
HIM AND OF HIS CAUSE *. Could we wifh a
feverer punifhment to our bittereft enemy †, than

---

* Dignus imperator legione Martiâ, digna legio impera-
tore. Cicero.

† Magne pater divûm, fævos punire tyrannos
Haud aliâ ratione velis! - - - - -
Virtutem videant, intabefcantque reliĉtâ.
PERS. Sat. iii. 35..

the

the complex fenfations arifing at once from the flagitious productions of thofe fcenes of horrour, and the moft complete difcomfiture of fuch audacious hectoring, fuch frantic impotence of malice?

———Ubi nunc Mezentius acer, et illa
Effera vis animi?

Mindful of the two great profeffors of the poetic art, lately fummoned for another purpofe; were the refufcitation of *one man* as eafy to me, as the tranfportation of *myriads* in Charon's wherry over that irremeable ftream is to certain minifters, I would call up the fhade of Homer to reprove Mr. Burke, with accents of fympathetic forrow over deluded zeal and proftituted homage, in return for fuch unfeafonable and outrageous panegyric:

Ατρειδη, ποιον σε επος φυγεν ερκος οδοντων;

And the fame vivifying caduceus fhould fummon Virgil from the bowers of Elyfium, to addrefs the incomparable fubject of the fame panegyric, on his political wifdom and fuccefs:

Ah! Corydon! Corydon! quæ te dementia cepit?

And with this diftribution of poetic juftice, I clofe the prefent feries of my remarks.

C   " They

" They unplumb the dead for bullets to
" affaffinate the living."

I felect for animadverfion but this little claufe
only, from one of the fublimeft invectives that
was ever poured forth by the phrenzy of irritated
genius from the fount of eloquence. Oh! that
fuch fplendid diction, fuch profufion of living
imagery, fuch vigour of conception, fuch fertility
of fancy, fuch magnificence of compofition,

" Thoughts that breathe, and words that burn,"

were mantled in the facred habiliments of Truth!

> A fairer perfon loft not heaven: he feem'd
> For dignity compos'd, and high exploit:
> But all was falfe and hollow; though his tongue
> Dropt manna, and could make the worfe appear
> The better reafon.

Now let us previoufly ftate the circumftances
of relation between the allied powers and the
French, to affift our judgement on this bold
charge of *affaffination* againft the detefted republicans.

A populous and powerful nation refolve on a
new modification of their government, and limit
the regal power by certain reftrictions deemed
favourable,

favourable, in the opinion of the nation at large,
to the liberties and happinefs of the fubject.
This monarch, fo conftituted, becomes unfaithful
to engagements, accepted with all the formalities
of public affent in the prefence of the people.
He is deprived of his office for this breach of
honour and of honefty. Now, whether this fovereign were wrongfully difplaced, or with juftice ;
whether this people conducted their proceedings
with rigorous propriety and from pure motives,
or with a violence and fiercenefs of ufurpation,
reprehenfible in any fuppofeable degree you
pleafe ; is it poffible for any man, not cankered
by the vileft peculation, not giddy with ambitious
projects, not frantic with intemperance of paffion ; to maintain, by fober argument, a right of
interference with the internal œconomy of this
country, on the part of any foreign potentate
whatever? Are then, indeed, the French juftly
deemed *affaffins*, if they repel by force the fanguinary plunderers and invaders of their terri-
tory, who threaten themfelves with flavery, their
leaders with deftruction, and their capital with
the lawlefs vengeance of a ruffian foldiery?
Nay, are thefe people not rather authorifed
(I fpeak after the manner of men, and upon the
profeffed theories of national politics in the
prefent profligacy of human governments) to

treat

treat thofe fpoilers, as an individual would treat
the murderer, who broke into hi., houfe to butcher
himfelf and family, and to fpoil his goods?
" May he that taketh up the fword, perifh by
" the fword !" I never could contemplate, I
freely acknowledge, for myfelf, the conduct of
the confederated league in any other point of
view than that, prefented in this ftatement ; and
had thefe bloody ravagers,

" Who fhut the gates of mercy on mankind,"

been themfelves cut off, root and branch, without
commiferation, by the enraged fwords of the
republicans ; I fhould have pronounced over their
baptifm of death the fentence of the Jewifh
captain : " Your blood be upon your own head !
" they are guiltlefs !"

———————— neque enim lex æquior ulla
Quam necis artifices arte perire fuâ.

Few tears of pity trickled down, few fighs of
compaffion were breathed out, while Phalaris
was bellowing the pangs of death in his own
bull.

Upon the whole, nothing now remains but for
my Lord Grenville, this Anak among ftatefmen,
this

this *Lucifer* among the twinkling drops of the
political hemisphere, to prepare courtly smiles
and phrases of benignity for a fraternal embrace
of an ambassador from those execrable regicides,
whom he has reviled with every species of
contumelious calumny, " foaming out it's own
" shame," in a stile of the coarseft possible vul-
garity, that could be raked from the finks of
Billingsgate. For myself, who have exulted in
the successes of the French, and the difgrace of
their insolent and odious foes, with a keenness of
transport not to be defcribed, I have been long
prepared to hail the triumphant entry of a
republican representative ; and shall exclaim,
with equal sincerity and rapture,

> Dicite, Io Pæan! et Io, bis dicite, Pæan!
>
> Oh! may I live to hail that glorious day,
> And sing loud Pæans through the crouded way!

Such a determination, therefore, as this upon
the present case, which dignifies *real murderers*
with the title of religious champions, and com-
mendable vindicators of peace and order, whilst
it calumniates the defenders of their country,
their property and their lives, with the atrocious
character of *affassins*; is one of those monstrous
perverfities, which degrade the species itself, and

approxi-

approximate to a perfect brutalization of rationality.

As for our author's " fanctuary of the tomb," and " his immunities of the dead," &c. thefe are the canting whimfies of a wild and gloomy imagination; the hypertragical whinings of puerile fuperftition ; the doatings of the nurfe, and the bugbears of the infant. Surely the utilities of the living will form the concern of reafonable men ; not the inexplicable confolations of the dead.

Id cinerem, aut manes credis curare fepultos?
For all is calm in that eternal fleep:
There Grief forgets to groan, and Love to weep.

At Shelford, near Nottingham, is the burial-vault of the Earls of Chefterfield. Some years ago, the fexton of that church, who was a tailor by trade, violated " the fanctuary of the tomb," by *cabbaging* flices of red velvet from the coffins of the noble fleepers, and felling them for *coat-collars* to his cuftomers. The whole parifh was furprifed at the quantity of red capes flaunting through the village, and illuminating the country round. At length the vicar, a fagacious and pious man ! traced the caufe of thefe flaming exhibitions ; and wrote, in terms of the moft

piteous

piteous horrour and lamentation, to the late Earl upon the fubject of fuch terrific and unhallowed depredation. The witty nobleman adminiftered ghoftly comfort to his vicar; exhorted him to moderate the exceffes of his forrow; and to join rather with himfelf in admiring and commending the provident ingenuity of the tailor, for bringing into light and employing ufefully what himfelf and his anceftors had configned to eternal dark-nefs and decay.

What our author next advances, here and throughout his pamphlet, of a perfonal nature merely, in juftification of his penfion, is in moft refpects fo reafonable, and is altogether conveyed in fuch melting ftrains of pathetic eloquence, as might difarm even Malice and Antipathy them felves of a wifh to cenfure. By me at leaft, the facred forrows of true genius, and the difconfo-late lamentations of an afflicted father, fhall be regarded, not with refpect only, but with re-verence. I have no wifh but to counteract the pernicious tendency of political extravagances and abfurdities; and hope, with a warmth of fincerity not exceeded by his deareft friends, that this fun of glory, through a gradual and mild decline, may finally fet in peace.

As

As to the penfion of Mr. Burke, if the prefent minifters, or any other fet of men, had come forward to the parliament and the public, in a tone, frank, and manly, and explicit: " Mr. Burke, " for a confiderable portion of his life, has de- " voted, in his fenatorial capacity, thofe talents " and accomplifhments,

" Of which all Europe rings from fide to fide,"

" to the fervice of the ftate, and has benefited his " country in fome moft important inftances : it " is our wifh to recompenfe the merits of fo great " a man, and to provide for the repofe of his " declining years, in a public remuneration, " fanctioned by the fuffrage of his country ; and " we apply to that country for this purpofe :"— if, I fay, a propofal of fuch a nature had been made, and in fome fuch manner, no man, I will venture to fay, would have hinted a fingle fufpi- cion of diflike. All parties and defcriptions would have joined in their applaufe of a meafure, apportioned with difcretion, not lefs honourable to the donors, than the fubject of it : nor would the Duke of Bedford and the Earl of Lauderdale, I am bold to affirm, been among the laft with their expreffions of affent, and contributions of efteem. It was the clandeftine management and myfterious fecrefy of this tranfaction, not unac-
companied

companied by no unreasonable presumption of
the wages of apostasy, that justly excited the
generous sensations of these noble persons;
sympathising in a spirit of the purest patriotism
for their exhausted country, and gloriously stand-
ing forth as the advocates of œconomy amidst the
unbounded prodigalities of ministerial corruption *.

That suspicion of desertion from the cause of
liberty, as not wholly coincident and commensu-
rate with conviction, on which I have just touched,
was but too powerfully aided by a display of
frantic vehemence (characteristic in many in-
stances of proselyte imposture, which endeavours
to atone for it's former obliquities by an inordi-
nate shew of zeal in support of it's adopted
faction) and a most callous obduracy to the
tender sensibilities of former friendship: an
obduracy, as I was informed by a friend to the
minister and a spectator of this extraordinary
scene, that affected the whole assembly with
unspeakable disgust and horrour at the victim of
such wretched passion; and imprinted more
deeply on the heart of every observer their love and
veneration for the generous affections of Mr. Fox.

* Fortunati ambo! si quid mea carmina possunt,
Nulla dies unquam memori vos eximet ævo.

Mr.

Mr. Burke himſelf ſhould have diſdained the myſticiſm and chicanery of ſuch paltry inſtruments. He ſhould have felt his life diſgraced, his endowments diſparaged, and his motives expoſeable to the moſt legitimate imputations of intereſted accommodation, by accepting on ſuch terms the bounty of men, who ſeem deſirous of ſeducing converts, only to diſgrace them:

" Hate ſtronger under ſhew of love well-feign'd:"

who join with charlatanical impoſture the hardneſſes of inhumanity: who forgive the heterodoxies of their new aſſociates, to inſure and precipitate their ruin, under the ſemblance of reconciliation and benignity. They preſent a branch of myrtle, but under the leaves is a poiſoned dagger.

Exiſting circumſtances have been growing for ſome time paſt rather too momentous for jocularity; otherwiſe, as Cicero ſomewhere expreſſes his ſurpriſe, that one *augur*, when he meets another, can forbear laughing in his face; ſo I have often wondered, that our *ſtate-augurs* can with-hold a ſmile of gaiety at each other, from a conſciouſneſs of the grand *humbug*, which they are carrying on with ſuch complete ſucceſs; cajoling the country, to enrich themſelves. Their conduct reminds me of a pleaſant paſſage in the works of

Pope,

Pope, which might indeed have taught me to ſuppreſs my ſurpriſe, by furniſhing a ſolution of my perplexity*:

" It is no wonder in an age of ſuch education
" and cuſtoms, that, as Thucydides ſays, *Robbing*
" was honoured, provided it were done with
" gallantry; and that the ancient poets made
" people queſtion one another as they ſailed,
" *if they were thieves?* as a thing, for which
" no one ought either to be ſcorned or up-
" braided!"

Thus far the poet.

" Aſtronomers have ſuppoſed, that if a certain
" comet, whoſe path interfeſted the ecliptick,
" had met the earth in ſome (I forget what) ſign,
" it would have whirled us along with it, in it's
" excentrick courſe, into God knows what re-
" gions of heat and cold. Had the portentous
" comet of the rights of man, (which ' from it's
' horrid hair ſhakes peſtilence, and war,' and
' with fear of change perplexes Monarchs')
" had that comet croſſed upon us in that internal
" ſtate of England, nothing human could have
" prevented our being irreſiſtibly hurried, out of

* Eſſay on Homer, ſect. iii

" the

" the highway of heaven, into all the vices,
" crimes, horrours, and miferies of the French
" revolution."

It is exceedingly to be lamented, that furious bi-
gotry in fome, fordid intereft, pride of rank, or fhal-
low prejudice in others, fhould obftruct or pervert
their view in the contemplation of the propofi-
tions involved in this quotation : or rather, that
with too much difcernment to be deluded themfelves, fuch numbers fhould be reduced by bad
paffions and dangerous purfuits to a falfe reprefen-
tation of the queftion for the purpofe of deceiv-
ing others, and converting their deluded votaries into the inftruments of their own ambition
and duplicity. The queftion never fubfifted between our prefent political condition, and the
exceffes fubfequent on the revolution in France.
The alternative truly lay, as every man of fenfe
muft inftantaneoufly perceive, and every honeft
mind as inftantaneoufly allow, between the
enormous fpoils of a licentious adminiftration,
and a temperate reform of corruptions, which
the moft unblufhing retainers of a court could
not but acknowledge to exift. It was the de-
termined refiftance of all reformations whatfoever, and a perfeverance on principle in a
fcheme of domination, which had deprived
the people of even the flender dependence hi-

7   therto

therto repofed on the mere fhadow of a r·p:e-
fentative conftitution, that made even moderate
reformers rife in their demands; and cruel im-
prifonments and arbitrary perfecutions, upon
the infufficient evidence of fpies and informers,
a circumftance of itfelf fufficient to blaft any
caufe, with a fucceffion of falfe alarms, and
fabricated plots, that drove multitudes from the
ftandard of monarchy to the ranks of republi-
canifm. I confidently affert, with the documents
of experience and the dictates of philofophy to
bear me out in this affertion, that fuch a refo-
lute rejection of all propofals for the melioration
of a fabric *, which, as human, muft neceffarily
want occafional repairs, and fhould improve with
improving man; I affert, that fuch a conduct was
probably effectual beyond all others, even that
fo ftrenuoufly oppofed, and fo tragically reviled,

---

* But *innovation* muft be refifted; which, however, as
my Lord Bacon obferves, Effay xxiv. is not more turbulent
than a " froward retention of cuftom:" which remark is
preceded by a fentence, fraught with intrinfic wifdom, and
extremely pertinent to the prefent difquifition :

" Surely every medicine is an innovation; and he, that
" will not apply new remedies, muft expect new evils: for
" Time is the greateft innovator; and, if Time of courfe
" alter things to the worfe, and Wifdom and Counfel fhall
" not alter them to the better, what fhall be the end ?"

to bring upon ourfelves " the vices, crimes, hor-
" rours, and miferies of the French revolution."
Such acutenefs of diftrefs, as is fuffered at this
moment from famine and other concomitant
difafters of the war, beyond all example and
almoft all endurance, by the inferior claffes of
fociety and the poor penfionaries of public
bounty, will naturally create a difcontent, in the
firft inftance, with the government, under which
they labour; and may ripen to a crifis of defpair,
that will involve itfelf and the whole fabric of
national exiftence in carnage and defolation.
Things cannot remain ftationary long. With the
prefent headftrong infatuation of our rulers, a
refuge will and muft be fought, in the regular
procefs of phyfical events, from the preffure of
infupportable calamity, either in the fiery ordeal
of revolution, or the hideous jaws of devouring
defpotifm:

—————Patet immani, et vafto refpeftat hiatu.

But from defpotifm, the prefent ftate of in-
telleftual advancement among mankind, in
union with the monftrous unconftitutional ufur-
pations of our rulers, and the unprincipled ex-
travagance of government expences, are likely,
I think,

I think, to fecure the nation, aided by the neighbouring influence of the French republic; not her arms, but the filent and tranquil operation of her principles on our character, our manners and, our policy: an imperceptible efficacious energy! which nothing can preclude, nothing can counteract, and nothing eventually refift. I fee that vaft, formidable empire, defcending, like the Nile, from the mountains of Æthiopia, circling with it's liquid arms the gay fabrics and the fpacious deferts of monarchy, ariftocracy, and ecclefiaftical ufurpation. I fee that deluge of mighty waters gradually fubfide into their wonted channel: I fee them flow with a majeftic tranquillity to the ocean, and all the traces of their former ravages obliterated by one extenfive and expanding Paradife of verdure, fertility, and beauty.

It is a fubject of grievous anxiety and of truly portentous apprehenfion, nor in the leaft degree to us, who have devoted ourfelves to the noifelefs occupations of fequeftered literature,

——— ——— mutas agitare inglorius artes,

that ignorant and befotted ftatefmen, fwollen with ariftocratic haughtinefs, or intoxicated with
power,

power, fhould be paffively endured to play fuch
a defperate game of hazard with all that is valuable in a community; and to expofe a whole
empire to the lawlefs depredations of the moft
neceffitous and untutored of mankind. And
yet the probability of a cataftrophe, fo truly tre-
mendous even in idea, is growing daily more
and more prefumable, from our difaftrous perfeverance in meafures, commenced with infanity,
purfued with ferocity, and continued from defpair. Thefe are melancholy forebodings ; but
cannot be too earneftly inculcated, nor too feri-
oufly recommended to the full reflection of my
countrymen. The reception of fuch warnings
with ridicule, or difregard, will only add to my
prefumption of their validity, from that fingu-
lar felf-delufion and infenfate blindnefs, infeparable from the promoters of alarming revolutions
on the eve of their appearance. If the prime
actors in thefe fcenes of madnefs " were aware
" that fuch a thing might happen, fuch a thing
" never could happen :" their fears would fur-
mount their obftinacy, and lead them to relent,
in feafonable conceffions, and gradual reformation.

Sed tamen effabor ; dictis dabit ipfa fidem res
Forfitan, et graviter terrarum motibus orbis

Omnia

Omnia conquaſſari in parvo tempore cernes.
Quod procul a nobis flectat fortuna gubernans;
Et ratio potius, quam res perſuadeat ipſa
Succidere horriſono poſſe omnia victa fragore.

Alaſs! the extravagant rampancy of haughty
rulers is but too apt to regard the maſs of mankind as beaſts of burden, brought into the world
with bridles in their mouths, and ſaddles on
their backs, ready to be ridden with whip and
ſpur by the nurſlings of royalty, the deſcendents
of nobility, and the ſable ſucceſſors of the order of Melchiſedech!

The remainder of this extraordinary pam-
phlet conſiſts of *five* ſeveral diviſions. In the *firſt*
is contained a ſtatement and vindication of the
writer's political exertions in the ſervice of his
country, with a detail of the difficulties, oppo-
ſed to his projects, from the prejudices of indi-
viduals and the peculiar embarraſſments of the
times. Such an air of generous ſelf-eſtimation,
but attempered with modeſty; ſuch an appearance of ſincerity, that diſdains a ſurrender of
it's own worth to the ſuggeſtions of falſe ſhame,
pervades this diviſion, as impreſſes on the face of
the narrative a ſtamp of authenticity, that will
enſure it's currency with diſpaſſiorate and can-
did readers. I myſelf at leaſt both wiſh it, and

D   believe

believe it, to be true. A *second* portion is employed on the Duke of Bedford and other particulars connected with him. A *third* is confecrated to the dirge of parental piety over a fon of his fondeft love. Here indeed are breathed the fighs of immortality! Here are poured, in forrowful profufion,

Thofe tears eternal, that embalm the dead !

A *fourth* divifion fulminates a ftorm of invective, black and loud, upon the revolutionifts of France; and the laft is occupied in the illuftration of Lord Kepple's character: a moft ftriking eulogy, fuch as could fcarcely have been hoped from the fondeft friendfhip of this inimitable artift, on his magnanimity, his abilities, and his private and public virtues. On *two* of thefe topics, I fhall prefume to fubjoin a few free remarks; after premifing, that the entire compofition rolls forward in a flood of fire, deep, flaming, and impetuous; involving every object within the vaft embrace of it's expanfion in one general conflagration. On the French revolution in particular, which lays every energy of his writhing fpirit on the rack of agony, his exertions are in a ftile of terrible fublimity, that thrills to the very marrow of the foul with a pleafing horrour :
a fub-

a fublimity, in my eftimation, without a parallel
in the repofitories of mortal eloquence.

Qui genus humanum ingenio fuperavit * !

But, as eloquence is no convertible term for
either truth or candour, when we feel our fouls
difenchanted by time and reflection from the
forceries of the tongue ; let us find leifure for
a difinterefted appeal from the impetuofity of
paffion to the fobriety of judgement; and confider, whether his remarks on the Duke of Bedford be compatible either with Truth, with Honour, or with Virtue.

As no circumftances and connections of my
life have introduced me to an experimental
knowledge of this noble perfon, (though, if I
were inclined to expatiate beyond my practical
information, I could extol one tranfcendent ex-
cellence upon the higheft credibility, and cf

---

* My commendations here, and elfewhere, muft be un-
derftood to refpect the *general fpirit* of the fentiments, and
the *abfolute* vigour and richnefs of expreffion ; not the *col-
location* of the words, or the arrangement of the claufes.
For in thefe refpects there are many unchaftifed impropie-
ties of grammar and conftruction ; there is much flovenli-
nefs and frequent ambiguity ; the refult, perhaps, of hafte
and negligence. In thefe particulars, Mr. Burke can fupport no competition with the beft writers of antiquity.

which

which my mind from the nature of the evidence
is perfectly affured :

Vivet extento Proculeius ævo,
Notus in fratres animi paterni :

without any conviction that will authorife on my
part the imputation of a fingle vice) I fhall
reftrain myfelf within the circumference of his
public character, and defcant on thofe overt
acts of political exertion, notorious to the world
at large.

And here furely an ingenuous obferver will
find ample materials for the pureft praife, and
bid defiance at the fame time to all fufpicion of
infinuating artifice and interefted adulation.

In the midft of a predominant confternation,
that has befotted the intellects of nobility, and
perverted the organs of their intellectual fight, in
confequence of a difpofition to behold the fun of
truth, broken and diftorted on the troubled waters of Gallic fury ; the Duke of Bedford has
preferved his mind in a calm of difpaffionate
neutrality : his feelings have continued without
diftemper, and his perfpicacity unclouded. He,
doubtlefs, with all the children of Virtue and
Benevolence and Senfibility, has viewed with

fenfations

fenfations of the deepeft anguifh, with fhudder-
ing nerves and with a bleeding heart, the fe-
rocious atrocities of that unhappy people ; atrocities, unexampled, I believe, in the fanguinary
egifter of human crimes ; atrocities, on which
to dwell with deliberate contemplation were an
infupportable agony of fpirit.

—— cui non conrepunt membra pavore ?

But his magnanimity and difcernment have con-
fpired to inftruct him, how to feparate the
actors from the *caufe* ; to diftinguifh the genuine
philofophical confequences of radical reformation, from the local, national, and educational peculiarities of the reformers. *He* has been for-
tunate enough to difcover, with other intelligent,
unprejudiced, and honeft men, a variety of reafons, operative to thefe exceffes, unconnected
with the fevereft principles of equality ; reafons,
not effentially interwoven with the broadeft
fyftem of univerfal Liberty. The grievous op-
preffions of that people under the bloody rod
of their defpotic tafkmafters, requiring brick,
but furnifhing no ftraw ; an infolent and profli-
gate nobleffe, yet unmollified by poverty and
exile, abforbing the vital nutriment of the
country, fo that their fleece alone grew wet,
when all around them was drynefs and fterility :

D 3

grofs

grofs and defpicable mummeries of fuperftition at once the parent and the chiid of ignorance and vice, each producing and fpringing from the other with reciprocal operation: thefe, and other concurrent caufes, not difficult to develop and enumerate, with fome probably unknown to me, carried their untutored minds, once un-fettered and put in motion, under the impulfe alfo of their former fufferings, down the fteep of licentioufnefs and cruelty with accelerated pre-cipitation. To expect a well regulated politi-cal œconomy, without tumult, without violence, without bloodfhed, to eftablifh itfelf at once in fuch untoward circumftances, amidft fuch a conflict of difcordant fentiments, oppofing inte-refts, and un-illuminated prepoffeilions, is unphi-lofophical, and inconfequent; a folecifm in poli-tical reafoning difgraceful to the moft defpica-ble intellect, or the very excefs of inexperience and puerility. Immure a man in the gloomy receffes of a dungeon; where, for a fucceffion of years, no light, fave the cafual glimmerings of a ftar, or the pale glances of the moon, fhall render vifible the palpable darknefs, that environs him: tell me, will fuch an one be able to encounter the broad beam of day, and much lefs the meridian blazes of the fun, without giddinefs of brain and a tem-porary extinction of his fight? This, if I miftake not,

not, may be juftly deemed the condition of the
French at the crifis under contemplation. But
no peculiarities of this nature (or in an incom-
parably lefs degree) accompanied the ftate of
Englifh polity and manners, fo as to authorife an
indifcriminate abufe and horrour of French principles, upon a rational expectation of the fame
refult in this country, from fimilar efforts of reformers. A long twilight of liberty had prepared our eyes to meet the emergence of open
day without dizzinefs and ftupefaction. Though
the filthy fcum of human authority and hierar-
chical domination, with fome abfurdities of lefs
extenfive operation, ftill floated on the furface of
our religious fyftem, the groffer dregs of Popifh
corruption were effectually drawn off : Chriftianity was not confined to the mere externals of
oftentatious ceremony, but ferved as a trunk to
fupport and nourifh a rational morality, con-
necting itfelf with the bufineffes and bofoms of
mankind ; and our religion was generally regarded not as a vifionary myfticifm, and a cloak
for hypocrify and crimes, but as a rule of life.

Thefe are a few, amongft a multiplicity of
circumftances, that feemed a probable barrier
againft the dreadful effects, fo juftly abhorred,
·but fo irrationally apprehended here; circum-

ftances

ſtances that might be deemed to render us capable of reaping the fruits of reformation, without previouſly taſting the bitterneſs of the root.

Behold then, with this preliminary proviſion full before us, a ſpeƈtacle, viewed in all its dependencies and conneƈtions, of no ordinary grandeur. A young nobleman, of the higheſt rank, the moſt ſplendid anceſtry, and the ampleſt fortune, ſtanding aloof from nearly an univerſal panic of his peers, at a time when the baſeſt arts of miniſterial intrigue had deluded the public ſentiment into a confuſion of conſtitutional freedom with levelling democracy, and had made even an oppoſition to ſlaughter and devaſtation a ſource of obloquy and danger : behold him aſſerting with a firm deciſion of charaƈter, with prompt elocution, and cogent reaſoning, thoſe maxims of civil polity, that placed the Brunſwic family on the throne ; condemning with indignant energy the groſs depravity of miniſters ; and reprobating that ardent thirſt of war which appeared, from the fierceneſs of their threats and the envenomed acrimony of their malice, to admit of no abatement, but by quenching it's fervours in the inundation of a whole country with the blood of it's inhabitants. It were caſy to have exhibited this piƈture of ·

firmneſs,

firmnefs, and good fenfe, much more at length, and in all it's attitudes, if an obvious reafon, which refpeBs myfelf, did not fuggeft the prudence of forbearance on this occafion. But neither the whifpers of unmanly fhame, nor coward apprehenfion from a charge of adulation, fhall betray me into a real impropriety, by ftudying to avoid an imaginary indecorum ; nor fhall Mr. Burke, with all the fafcinations of his eloquence, feduce me from an high admiration and warm applaufe of the Duke of Bedford's conduct. From the fhield of ætherial temper, prefented by fuch public Virtue, fuch difinterefted Patriotifm, even the furious lance of that flower of chivalry, the weapon of mere mortal paffion, falls innoxious to the ground.

—— poftquam arma dei ad Vulcania ventum eft,
Mortalis mucro, glacies ceu futilis, iBu
Diffiluit : fulvâ refplendent fragmina arenâ.

To pafs over without notice thofe farcaftical afperities on royal grants and tranfmitted property, furely not perfeBly confiftent in an avowed champion of nobility ; and to difmifs unchaftifed thofe coarfeneffes of phrafeology, not very honourable, I think, to fuch exquifite elegance of tafte; I would afk fimply, is it decorous, is it generous, is it manly, is it *innocent*, to promote

an

an odium on the Duke of Bedford, from the
fuppofed frailties of his progenitors, and from
irrelative incidental peculiarities of their private
or political condition *? What high and copious
panegyric on the Duke, that through his remote
anceftors alone, his charaÆter fhould be deemed
vulnerable! And what a fatire is this extraneous
digreffion on the head and heart of Mr. Burke!
On his *head*, for attempting to affociate two
things fo totally unconnefted and diffimilar, as
prefent worth and antediluvian infirmities, with
an expeÆtation too of duping his readers by fuch
a flimfy artifice : on his *heart*, for a torrent of
impotent and inapplicable defamation, calcu-
lated to debauch the judgement and inflame the
malignant paffions of his readers.

" The Duke of Bedford conceives, that he is
" obliged to call the attention of the Houfe of
" Peers to his Majefty's grant to me, which he
" confiders is exceffive and out of all bounds."

And the Duke of Bedford is, I think, abun-
dantly juftifiable in this affertion, and deferving
of applaufe, for the fpirit, which prompted him
to make it. Mr. Burke! there muft be fome-

---

* Nobilis hic, quocunque venit de gramine. Juv.

thing

thing culpable, it fhould appear to me, either in
the difpolition, or the conduct, of a man of
letters, to wifh or require fo large a fum for the
fatisfaction of his exigencies. A philofopher,
like you, fhould have inured himfelf to circum-
fcribe his wants, and moderate every enjoyment
purely perfonal, with jealous circumfpeCtion and
a principled fcrupulolity.

> Quod fi quis verâ vitam ratione gubernet,
> Divitiæ grandes homini funt vivere parce
> Æquo animo.

Confider, I befeech you, how many ftudents,
not gifted indeed with a tythe of your genius,
but in learning and in labour not much inferiour,
your penfion would make affluently rich, and
happy to the fulleft extenfion of their defires.
Condefcend to inftitute for one moment a comparifon between your enormous grant, and the
rule of fufficiency prefcribed by one, well known
to you, for men of your intellectual and fublimed character :

> ————————— menfura tamen quæ
> Sufficiat censûs, si quis me confulat, edam :
> In quantum fitis, atque fames, et frigora pofcunt ;
> Quantum, Epicure, tibi parvis fuffecit in hortis ;
> Quantum Socratici ceperunt ante penates.

Make

Make this comparifon, I fay; and then judge
whether you have not difgraced yourfelf, the
caufe of letters, and the tenour of your life, by
the acceptance of fo vaft a fum, when multitudes of your deferving countrymen, from this
glorious war of order, of religion, and of humanity, are pining in diftrefs, unnoticed and unknown; fhivering with cold, and perifhing
with famine. Your perfonal dignity, that genius, that fcience, that ftore of literary accomplifhments, which are all likewife your's in ac-
cumulated meafure, " preffed down and running
" over;" have contracted, I fear, a ftain of in-
delible difhonour. Either you have never fuf-
ficiently impreffed on your mind that dignified
fentiment of Pythagoras,

$$\text{------} \pi\alpha\nu\tau\omega\nu \; \delta\varepsilon \; \mu\alpha\lambda\iota\sigma\tau' \; \alpha\iota\sigma\chi\upsilon\nu\varepsilon\nu \; \sigma\alpha\upsilon\tau\upsilon\nu \cdot$$

or you muft have fuffered a temporary rafure of
this invaluable maxim from the tablet of your
memory. You, of all mankind, fhould have
been aware, that even the benevolence of gra-
cious kings might confer but ignominy on EDMUND
BURKE. Reflect alfo, Sir! that it is a duty of
philofophers and Chriftians, to raife ourfelves,
after the utmoft capacity of our frail natures, to
a refemblance of the Divinity itfelf. " Be ye

6
" therefore

" therefore perfect, even as your Father, which
" is in heaven, is perfect." True greatness and
fuperiority of character confift in contracting the
fphere of our wants, and in the diminution of
their number. The man of feweft defires, and
thofe defires within the compafs of his own
abilities to fatisfy, exhibits the nobleft pattern
of genuine philofophy, and the clofeft approxima-
tion to fublimer natures. But the depraved tafte
of Mr. Burke may be concluded to regard with
more admiration " the glory of Solomon, than
" the lily of the field."

With refpect to Mr. Burke's renewed invectives on the French, they are virulent, they are
furious, they are infernal, to the utmoft capa-
bilities of language. But, whether thefe torrent
eruptions of outrageous zeal proclaim more
loudly the powers of the head, or the perverfities of the heart, is a problem beyond my materials of moral demonftration to refolve. To his
vigour of conception, his comprehenfion and
vivacity of thought, his energies of phrafe, his
accumulations of original and ftriking imagery,
it is difficult for conjecture to fix a limit : but
his acrimony, his phrenzies, his abfurdities, his
mifreprefentations, and his inconfiftencies, have
alfo certainly no bounds. This feems a parallel
cafe

cafe to that ftated by Sir Richard Steele between the hierarchy of Rome and the church of England: the one is infallible, and the other is never in the wrong. It is the cafe, with an exception of variation in their predominant accomplifhment, of immortal Marlborough, as eftimated by the poet of my affection:

> In each, how guilt and greatnefs equal ran;
> And all, that rais'd the hero, funk the man!

When this *Jupiter fulminans* of literature is difcharging all the artillery of heaven (as if it fhould be hell) againft France;

> Quicquid habent telorum armamentaria cœli;   Juv.

whilft he is darting from a black ftorm of wrath his thunder and his lightnings on the republicans; whilft he endeavours to difparage thefe fhattered victims of his vengeance by contrafting the fonorous vocabulary of "the *Turennes*, the "*Luxembourgs*, and the *Boufflers*," with the more humble and vulgar names of "the *Pichegru* and "*Jourdans*;" his impotence of paffion not only depraves his judgement *, but betrays his memory.

---

* Nitimini cohoneftare res turpes, atque, omnibus argutiarum modis pro rebus fubditis, verborum invertitis corrumpitisque

mory. Perhaps, the *Brunfwicks*, and the *Co-bourgs*, and the *Clairfayes*, and the *Wirtemburgs*, may found as big, and may have fought as well, but in much bloodier and more glorious fields, as thefe *Turennes*, *Luxembourgs*, and *Boufflers* : and yet the *Jourdans* and the *Pichegrus*, to the moft perfect contentment of my heart ;

——————— O ! colendi
Semper, et culti!

thefe ignoble fans-culottes, I fay, have exhibited, in thofe mighty heroes of nobility, a moft delectable exemplification of that folid and indifput-able maxim :

The man that fights, and runs away,
May live to fight another day.

What? Is not Mr. Burke aware, that it may be with *generalfhip*, as it is, and has often been, with *eloquence* and *learning* ?

——————— imâ ex plebe Quiritem
Facundum invenies : folet hic defendere caufas
Nobilis indocti : veniet de plebe togatâ,
Qui juris nodos et legum ænigmata folvat.

rumpitisque naturas ; atque, ut olim accidere male fanis fo-let, quorum turbida vis morbi fenfum atque intelligentiam depulit, confufa atque incerta jactatis, et inania per rerum figmenta bacchamini. ARNOBIUS.

When

When Marſhal Tallard was riding with the Duke of Marlborough in his carriage, after the victory of Blenheim; " My Lord Duke," ſays the Marſhal, " you have beaten to-day the beſt " troops in the world." " *I hope,*" replied the Duke, " *you except thoſe who have had the honour* " *of beating them.*"

Let us be inſulted no more with ſuch boiſterous nothingneſs, with ſuch ineffably contemptible bombaſt. Our own eyes tell us in the *Grenvilles* and the *Pitts,* that *heaven-born miniſters* exiſt: and why not *generals* of the ſame ætherial extraction?

" However, let his Grace think as he may of " my demerits with regard to a war with regi " cide, he will find my guilt confined to that " alone. He never ſhall, with the ſmalleſt co " lour of reaſon, accuſe me of being the au " thor of a peace with regicide."

If I, a *ſwiniſh plebeian,* may be allowed to perſonate Herod the *king,* for a ſingle moment, " This is Paul unregenerate, *breathing out threat-* " *enings and ſlaughter,* riſen from the dead." What a frightful contraſt have we here, between *Jeſus of Nazareth,* and *Edmund Burke!* When
Chriſt

Chrift came into the world, *peace* was *fung** :
when he left the world, *peace* was *bequeathed†*.
But War, bloody, favage, unrelenting, extermi-
nating War,

> ———— horrid king! befmeared with blood
> Of human facrifice, and parents' tears—

is the frantic cry, the uniform proclamation, of
this infatuated, queftionable prophet of ariftocracy:

> War firft, war laft, war midft, and without end ‡.

A peace with *regicides!* What then would Mr.
Burke have thought, had he been a French-
man, of a peace with HOMICIDES? If a man
were compelled to make his horrid choice, would
he not prefer for himfelf the fingle decapitation
of poor unhappy Louis, to fwelling with his war-
whoop that terrific yell, which was the prelude
to the maffacre, perhaps, of no lefs than TWO

---

* Luke ii. 13, 14.　　　　† John xiv. 27.

‡ We may reprefent to our imaginations this fpurious
difciple of a meek and lowly Saviour, pouring forth his
devotional ejaculations to his grim idol, as he is a fcholar, in
terms fomething like the following:

Ω Πολεμε, κτεσιν Σατανα τεκ☽, ὃ πιτε σειο
Λησομαι, αρχομεν☽, ἐδ᾽ αναπαυομεν☽·
Αλλ᾽ αιει πρωτον τε, και ἱστατον, εν τε μεσοισιν
Αιτω· συ δ᾽ εμευ κλιθι, και εσθλα διδε.

E　　　　　　　　MILLIONS

MILLIONS of human beings? many of them, in
their individual capacity, of more worth than all
the kings in Chriſtendom ; and to whom life was
as ſweet and valuable *, as .to the proudeſt
monarch on a throne. Surely, ſurely, Mr. Burke!
it is better that *one axe* ſhould be uncaſed for a
few ſolitary victims of royal birth, than that
myriads of ſwords ſhould leap from their ſcab-
bards for the aſſaſſination of ſuch multitudes of
men.

Though I ſpeak thus freely, under the irre-
ſiſtible incentives of undiſputed and important
truths, I feel myſelf, and ſhall be deemed ſincere
by thoſe who know me, as deeply impreſſed by
the unparalleled calamities of that unhappy
family, as the generality of ſuſceptible minds. But
for thoſe advocates of blood, who could rejoice
over the deſtruction of their fellow-creatures, and
detail, with exaggerated malignity, the ſlaugh-
ters of the French in their gazettes, with all the
exultation of a Cyclops, belching the crudities
of human victims, and beſmeared with their
gore:—for beings like theſe, I ſay, to talk of *their*

* Ου γαρ εμοι ψυχης ανταξιον, ɤɩ' οσα φασιν
Ιλιον εκτησθαι——— Hom. Il. ix. 401.
end the whole of that divine paſſage.

compaſſion

compaſſion for Louis and his family, and *their*
deteſtation of the cruelties exercifed upon
them *, is the moſt audacious infult on the common fenfe and feelings of humanity within my
knowledge. After a complexion of abfurd in-
confiſtency, not lefs odious and contemptible,
are the commendations lavifhed on Mr. Wilber-
force for his exertions in behalf of flavery : that
politico-theological Satyr! who with one breath
can cool the burning anguifh of the African, and
with another, in the fame inſtant, can blaſt the
fpring from the year†, by giving his vote to an
abandoned miniſter for the extirpation of half the
youth of Europe by the fword! Men, like
thefe, are poffeffed (it is impoffible!) of no true,
fubftantial, fundamental religion whatfoever,
feated either in the underſtanding or the heart.
Their God is Moloch; their Chriſt, a fanatic
juggler; their faith, credulity; their religion, a

---

* Jam 'dudum me fateor, reputantem mecum in animo
rerum hujufcemodi monſtra, folitum effe mirari, audere vos
dicere quenquam ex his atheum, irreligiofum, facrilegum :
cum, fi verum fiat atque habeatur examen, nullos quam vos
magis hujufcemodi par fit appellationibus nuncupari.

                                              ARNOBIUS.

† ——ὡς Περικλης εφη, την νεοτητα, την απολομενην εν τῳ
πολεμῳ, ουτως ηφανισθαι εκ της πολεως, ὡς περ ει τις το εαρ εκ
τε ενιαυτε εξελοι.

            DION. HAL. *de Demoſt. et Ariſtot. ſect.* 8.

ceremonial

ceremonial of paltry fervices; and their morality, a complication of all unrighteoufnefs. They are indeed the bittereft enemies of Jefus, and the groffeft libel on his difpenfation. '

I now clofe thefe ftrictures with a fimple declaration that, whatever conclufion any reader may choofe to infer from the fpirit of this pamphlet, not one fyllable throughout was prompted by native malignity of heart; not one fentiment was thrown off by the effervefcence of malevolent emotion againft Mr. Burke, or any being that exifts: fo help me God! My fole incentive was, an unmingled antipathy to vice; an antipathy which I will manifeft, unfeduced by intereft, and unterrified by confequences, 'till the touch of Death fhall chill the brain that dictates, and ftiffen the hand that executes, together. Part of this declaration the fuffrage of my friends will ratify; my condition in life proclaims the reft.

Hackney, Feb. 28, 1796.

THE END.

THE
FOLLOWING WORKS
BY THE SAME
AUTHOR.

1. A New Tranflation of St. Matthew's Gofpel, with a Commentary and Notes, 4to. *boards*, 10s. 6d.
2. The Evidences of Chriftianity, or Remarks on the Excellency, Purity, and Character of the Chriftian Religion, *fecond edit.* much enlarged, *boards*, 4s. 6d. 1793.
3. An Enquiry into the Opinions of Chriftian Writers of the firft Centuries, concerning the Perfon of Jefus Chrift, 1784, 8vo. *boards*, 4s.
4. An Effay on Infpiration, confidered chiefly with refpect to the Evangelifts, 1781, 2s. 6d.
5. Four Marks of Antichrift, 1s.
6. A Sermon preached at Richmond, in Surry, July 29, 1784, a public Thankfgiving-Day, 6d.
7. Remarks on Dr. Horfley's Ordination Sermon, in a Letter to the Bifhop of Gloucefter, 1788, 4d.
8. A New Tranflation of thofe Parts only of the New Teftament which are wrongly tranflated in our common Verfion, 2s. 6d. 1789.
9. A Short Enquiry into the Expediency and Propriety of Public or Social Worfhip, *third edit.* 1s. 6d. 1792.
10. Short Strictures on Dr. Prieftley's Letter to a Young Man, concerning Mr. Wakefield's Treatife on Public Worfhip, 1792, 6d.
11. A General Reply to the Arguments againft the Enquiry into Public Worfhip, 1792, 6d.
12. A Letter to the Lord Bifhop of St. David's, on Occafion of a Pamphlet relating to the Liturgy of the Church of England, afcribed to him, 1s. 1790.
13. An Examination of Thomas Paine's Age of Reafon: the 2d edition, corrected and enlarged: with an Appendix to David Andrews, in Defence of Chriftianity, 1794, 2s.
14. An Examination of the Second Part of the fame Writer, 1795. 1s. 6d.
15. The Spirit of Chriftianity, compared with the Spirit of the Times. An improved edition, 1s. 1794.
16. The Poems of Mr. Gray, with Notes. 3s. 6d.

17. Remarks

17. Remarks on the General Orders given by the Duke of York to his Army on July 7th, 1794, respecting the Decree of the French Convention to give no Quarter to the British and Hanoverians. 1s. 1794.
18. The Works of Alexander Pope, Esq. with notes, vol. 1. 6s. or on fine paper, 8s. 1794.
19. Observations on Pope, vol. 2. 7s. 1796.
20. A Translation of the New Testament, 2 vols. 8vo. second edition, 16s. *in boards.*
21. Poetical Translations from Horace, Virgil, Juvenal, Lucretius, the Greek Anthologia, and the Psalms: *boards*, 2s. 6d. *fine paper*, 4s. 1795.
22. Silva Critica, five in auctores sacros profanosque Commentarius Philologus. Cantabrigiæ, typis et sumptibus Academicis, 1789, 3s. 6d.
23. Silva Critica, pars II. 1790, 3s. 6d.
24. Silva Critica, pars III. 1792, 3s. 6d.
25. Silva Critica, pars IV. 1793, 5s.
26. Silva Critica, pars V. 1795, 3s. 6d.
27. Virgilii Maronis Georgicôn libri IV. 1788, 3s. 6d.
28. Poëmata, Latine partim scripta, partim reddita, quibus accedunt quædam in Q. Horatium Flaccum Observationes Criticæ, 4to. *sewed*, 2s. 1776.
29. Horatii Opera, nitidissime impressa, duobus tomis. 10s. 6d. 1794.
30. Tragœdiarum Græcarum delectus; Æschyli Eumenides; Sophoclis Trachiniæ et Philoctetes; et Euripidis Hercules Furens, Alcestis, et Ion. 2 tom. 8vo. 14s. chartâ majore, 1l. 11s. 6d.
31. Bionis et Moschi quæ supersunt, emendáta et illustrata, formâ minóre, 3s. 6d. majore, 10s. 6d. 1795.
32. P. Virgilii Máronis Opera, duobus tomis, formâ minore, 12s. majore, 1l. 11s. 6d. 4to.

In the Press.

Lucretii Opera, longe emendatiora, et copiosis notis illustrata, cum Bentleii etiam Commentariis nondum editis, in 4to. N. B. Exemplaria perpauca, nitore summo adornata, excudentur.

In a few Weeks will be published,

The Iliad and Odyssey of Pope, with Notes critical and illustrative. in 9 volumes, 8vo.